VENETIAN RAPIER

VENETIAN RAPIER

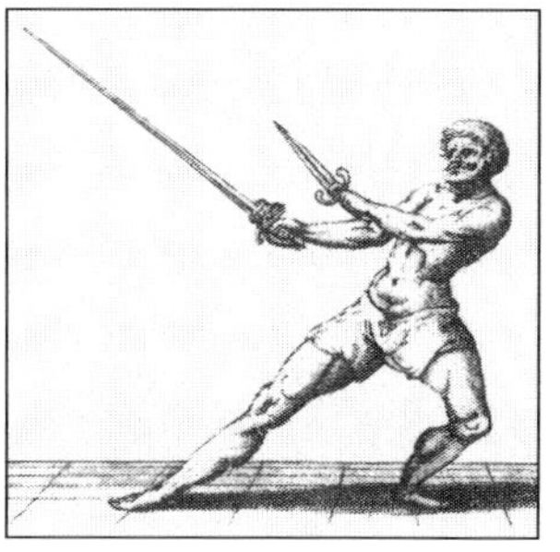

The School, or Salle

NICOLETTO GIGANTI'S 1606 RAPIER FENCING CURRICULUM

with New Introduction, Complete Text Translation, and Original Illustrations

By

Tom Leoni

Freelance Academy Press, Inc.
www.FreelanceAcademyPress.com

Freelance Academy Press, Inc., Wheaton, IL 60189
www.freelanceacademypress.com

Printed in the United States of America
by Publishers' Graphics

19 18 17 16 15 14 13 12 11 10   1 2 3 4 5

ISBN 978-0-9825911-2-3

Library of Congress Control Number: 2010920782

Contents

Acknowledgments

I'd like to thank my editing team for helping me improve this book: Adam Velez, Chris Vail, Kari Carlson, Terry Tindill, Tim Lyon, and Tracy Kopecky. It's a rare piece of good luck to have such a talented team on your side, made of knowledgeable individuals who are as good with the pen as they are with the sword.

Also a big thanks to Steve Reich for his invaluable help with the illustrations.

Introduction

Become proficient in the actions in Giganti's lessons and you can call yourself a rapierist.

As a rapier teacher, I am often asked to present a curriculum that is at one time concise, complete, consistent and authentic. *Concise* meaning pared down to the fundamental defensive and offensive actions; *complete* meaning thorough in mechanical, technical and tactical terms—as well as presenting a useful variety in repertoire; *consistent* meaning internally contradiction-free and in line with the tradition; and *authentic* meaning coming straight from a period Master.

Nicoletto Giganti is one of two prominent 17th-century rapier Masters offering this type of curriculum with his 1606 text *The School, or Salle*. The other is Bondi' di Mazo, who published a book on rapier with a similar pedagogical template ninety years later. Both Masters are Venetian, and there is a temptation to hypothesize that the pedagogy presented by these Masters would have been peculiar to the *Serenissima Repubblica*.

One thing that is far from the realm of speculation is that Giganti's text is most definitely a curriculum, as opposed to the formal and systematic treatises of Masters like Fabris and Marcelli.[1] Besides Giganti's telltale pedagogical terseness, there are two other reasons for me to make this statement. First, the subtitle to the book states explicitly that the work is to be used by swordsmanship students to "practice and become proficient in the discipline of arms." Then, he overtly calls the illustrated text units making up his book "lessons" to be "practiced with assiduity."

I don't need to wax poetic pointing out the value of a swordsmanship text such as Giganti's. As far as benefits go, having a rapier curriculum that modern enthusiasts can follow in the same order as martial artists four centuries ago is as self-explanatory as it gets.

I will instead keep speaking as a martial artist and offer modern rapier students enough tools to make the most out of Giganti's text and illustrations for training purposes. But first, a little background about Venice.

---

1 The two Masters mentioned are: Salvator Fabris, who published his monumental rapier treatise *Lo Schermo, overo Scienza d' Arme* in Copenhagen in 1606; and Francesco Antonio Marcelli, who codified his father's and uncle's teachings in the 1686 treatise *Regole della Scherma*, published in Rome.

Although as beautiful and seemingly delicate as lace, Venice has rightfully earned the reputation of a strong and martially pragmatic city-state. The Republic proudly endured for 1,070 years, unconquered until Napoleon's juggernaut forced her to bow her head in 1797; but even then, she bowed her head to a proto-industrial military complex several times the size of what she could ever field. One of the reasons for its successful history is that, not unlike Switzerland, Venice had a long-established tradition of a standing military ready to mobilize at a moment's notice. The city was renowned for producing skillful crossbowmen, swordsmen, sailors and even cavalry—the latter mostly belonging to the nobility. Equally famous were the Slavic mercenaries (*Schiavoni*) and the marines (*ultramarini*), recruited from nearby Dalmatia and Istria.

The Veneto region (the Northeastern part of Italy), with the great university-town of Padua being only a few miles away from Venice, was a prolific breeding ground of fencing Masters who attracted young and earnest students from all over Europe. Salvator Fabris and Francesco Alfieri were prominent Masters who made the Veneto famous for their fencing instruction. Also, weapon and armor makers from the area worked with the excellent iron ore from Eastern Lombardy, and used their ingenuity to create uniquely Venetian weapons. Examples of these are the distinct 15th-century broadswords, the Schiavona, the crab-claw hilted swords and rapiers, and many others.

Martial exercise was heartily encouraged and sometimes even mandated. A vestige of this tradition can be seen even today in the historic regattas, which started as ways to make rowers stronger and more skilled, since Venice only employed free citizens to man her war galleys.

This is the rich backdrop of Nicoletto Giganti's activity as a teacher and martial artist.

What We Know about Giganti

Nicoletto Giganti was probably born around 1550 or 1560, and as stated on his portrait in the book's frontispiece, he was Venetian. The pieces of data I have found in contemporary sources point to the fact that he did not die before 1622, that he may have spent parts of his life abroad, and that other notable Masters in the Italian tradition laud him as a worthy instructor. Let us proceed chronologically.

Nicoletto Giganti, as portrayed on the frontispiece of *The School, or Salle*, 1606.

We know by his own words that the 1606 work is his first, as he states more than once. It was not uncommon for a Master to wait until mid-life before publishing a book on swordsmanship, as did Salvator Fabris, in his early sixties, and Ridolfo Capoferro,[2] in his early fifties.

We know that, although writing on the sword we now call "rapier," he chooses to be immortalized holding a *spadone*, the massive two-handed sword used mostly in Italy, Germany,

2 Author of the treatise *Gran Simulacro dell' Arte e dell' Uso della Scherma*, Siena, 1610.

and the Iberian Peninsula. This suggests he would have been a well-rounded martial artist, as indeed were other prominent Masters of his time. We also know that as he writes this book, he plans on writing more in the future. And according to at least one source, he did.

Johann Joachim Hynitzsch, who in 1676 devotedly translated Fabris' rapier treatise into German, accuses Giganti of publishing Book II of Fabris' work under his own name in 1622, after translating it (or having it translated) into French and German parallel text. I have very recently heard accounts of this book's surfacing; the accusation of plagiarism may indeed be founded, and I may have further details upon a subsequent edition of this book.

Hynitzsch adds that besides being a plagiarist, Giganti betrays a lack of understanding of the art of fencing. However, the German gives no significant details to substantiate this last accusation. As for us, 400 years later, we don't have Fabris, his students and other giants of the rapier to use as a benchmark to even hazard passing judgment on a dead tradition.

But fortunately for Giganti and his posthumous reputation, one of the finest Masters in 17th-century Italy names him as one of two authors who, alone, "come close to the truth of the rules [of certain actions] and their finesse," speaking in particular of the lunge.[3]

In the 19th and early 20th centuries, prominent researchers of historical fencing shower lavish praise on Giganti. For instance, Jacopo Gelli proclaims Giganti to be a glorious pillar of the Italian fencing tradition, again pointing in particular to his description of the lunge, and using his teachings as the umpteenth pretext to direct a salvo at the Neapolitan school he so detested.[4]

I am notoriously skeptical about Victorian and Edwardian fencing historians, with their propensity to editorialize and to sometimes use the past creatively to bolster their pet side in contemporary *querelles*. But I am also of the opinion that Giganti is, at the very least, a fine martial teacher and, at most, one of the best resources that we moderns have to understand the rapier and how to practice it.

What We Know about Giganti's 1606 Book

The 95-page oblong book's entire title is *The School, or Salle, in which are represented various ways and means to defend and attack with single sword and sword and dagger; and whereby students may practice and become proficient in the discipline of arms.* It sees the light in 1606 in Venice, one of the European capitals of book-printing, from the presses of Giovanni Antonio and Jacopo de' Franceschi.

Dealing with sword alone and sword and dagger, the text is composed of self-contained chapters, almost all of which are accompanied by illustrations. The only attribution I have seen concerning the illustrations, 42 in number plus the portrait of the Master, is to the Bolognese engraver Edoardo Fialet.[5]

3 Francesco Antonio Marcelli, op. cit., page 69. The other Master lauded by Marcelli is Francesco Alfieri, author of several martial treatises including *La Scherma*, 1640.

4 J. Gelli, *Bibliografia Generale della Scherma*, Hoepli, Milan, 1890, pp 112 and ff.

5 J. Gelli, op. cit.

The illustrations match the texts with few exceptions, which I have footnoted with my own suggestions. The greatest exception is the stance of fencers while in guard: while the illustrations depict a wide stance, the text specifies more than once that the guard should feature a moderate stance so as to facilitate a longer lunge.

Apropos the illustrations, it has been suggested that the plates in Giganti, Capoferro and Alfieri may be variations of a common set (perhaps a royalty-free set), modified ad-hoc to fit the instruction of the respective authors. This is an interesting theory, and one to which I subscribe, although as of yet I have nothing but mere opinion to support it.

Going back to *The School, or Salle,* the work was reprinted in French and German parallel text in 1619 by De Zeter of Frankfurt. This edition, which I have, is complete and well-translated, and points to the fact that Giganti's work must have had some market outside of Italy. According to Gelli, there were a few more subsequent editions, including a 1628 Italian edition and a 1622 German edition.

Also according to Gelli, Giganti did fulfill his promise to write a subsequent book on single sword and sword with a variety of companion weapons; in 1608, an illustrated work to this effect was published in Italy by Fontana. To my knowledge, this work has not yet resurfaced.

Giganti's Voice and Language, and a Note on the Translation

The voice of Giganti is terse and pragmatic (plain style), which is consistent with what was thought to be best for an instructional work—especially a martial work. His line "let it not be said that I repeat myself unnecessarily" seems to have been his guiding principle while writing the book.

Giganti is also fairly consistent in his terminology, as a worthy instructor of any art should be.

As always in my translations of swordsmanship texts, I tried to bring to life not only the words, but also the style of the author. All the actions, concepts, terms and figures of speech have been translated into modern English as faithfully as possible with two languages that come from different roots.

Please note: a few concepts that Giganti explains with vague and inconsistent words, I have clarified with more common 17th-century rapier terms, such as "inside" and "outside," while leaving the meaning of the instruction intact. Any choice I have made to this effect is for one main purpose: to make the Master's words accessible to modern swordsmanship students.

Giganti and the Italian Tradition

There is nothing in Giganti's text that points to any substantial idiosyncrasies in the actions he presents or the mechanics he uses. What he describes is a distillation of the actions and the mechanics that can also be found in Fabris, Capoferro, Alfieri and other authors of his time.

The most salient exception is one of terminology: he does not name the four Italian guards and/or hand-positions. There is no prima, seconda, terza, or quarta in his text, although hand-positions can be understood rather easily through his words and illustrations.

What You Need to Know to Tackle Giganti

There is something to be said for the argument often heard in Western martial arts circles that swordsmanship books written centuries ago would have "been aimed at an audience already familiar with the concepts and actions—at least to some extent." How much is "some extent"? There is of course no way to answer this question, and perhaps the author himself would have found it hard to do so.

So, since I am speaking to a modern audience, I have decided to include a few concepts and definitions so that even less-experienced readers can better understand the actions in Giganti, construct drills out of his lessons, and ultimately enjoy his text more. Please bear in mind that this is necessarily concise and aimed at the fencer who is not familiar with these concepts; for any terms you may not understand, please refer to the glossary at the end of the book.

Also, please bear in mind that the following assumes a right-handed fencer.

What sword to use – Use any sword commonly referred to as "rapier," i.e., a single-handed, straight-bladed, two-edged sword with a hilt of varying complexity that enables you to place your index finger around the ricasso, i.e., the thick section of the blade just beyond the cross-guard (more on this in the section about gripping the sword). Although Giganti does not address length, any well-balanced rapier whose cross-guard stands as high as your navel will give you good results. I refer to the rapier as "sword" throughout the translation, since this is what Italian Masters called their weapon (*spada*).

Division of the blade – The blade is divided in two equal halves: *forte* (strong) and *debole* (weak). The forte is the half closest to your hand and is used for parrying. The debole is the other half and is used for offense. Some Masters divided the blade in different ways, but this will suffice. The blade also has a true edge and a false edge. The true edge is the edge facing the ground when you carry the sword sheathed at your side.

How to grip the sword – Grip the sword with your whole hand around the handle, and the index finger through the *incascio*.[6] Let your relaxed thumb rest on the tip of the index, achieving the grip called *a chiave serrata* (closed-key) by Italian Masters.

The four hand-positions – The four hand-positions or guards in Italian rapier are (assuming a right-handed fencer and the sword-point aimed at the opponent):

- The prima (first): hand at shoulder-level or higher, palm facing right, the sword's true edge pointing up
- The seconda (second): hand at shoulder-level, palm facing down, the sword's true edge pointing right

6 The *incascio* is the portion of the hilt between the hilt's front arm and the ricasso.

- The terza (third): hand lower than the shoulder (chest-level or lower), palm facing left, the sword's true edge pointing down
- The quarta (fourth): hand lower than the shoulder (chest-level or lower), palm facing up, the sword's true edge pointing left.

The three bastard hand positions – These are the intermediate positions between prima and seconda (called therefore prima-seconda), between seconda and terza (seconda-terza) and between terza and quarta (terza-quarta).

How to stand in guard – The main guard is the initial position in rapier fencing, although, as Giganti also specifies, it should quickly turn into a posture designed to counter the opponent's guard (counter-guard). Nevertheless, the guard should be practiced to become second nature, since it is the "neutral" position from which all other actions spring. The general Italian guard I teach, which is suitable for Giganti, is as follows:

- Start by standing erect looking at the opponent and your chest facing left, your right foot pointed at the opponent, your left foot pointed to your left and slightly back, forming with the right foot an obtuse angle, heels touching. Have your sword at your left side, as if in a scabbard; hold it against your hip with your left hand on the blade just under the hilt; and grip the sword with your right hand as described.
- "Unsheathe" your sword and point it at the opponent's face, with your hand in terza, your arm quite extended (but never locked) and your hilt approximately at the height of your solar plexus.
- Bring your front foot approximately one-and-a-half shoe-lengths forward along the same straight line between you and the opponent, right knee almost straight. Keep most of your weight on the left foot by gently bending your left leg and slightly tilting your body back, chest still facing left. Hold your head also slightly back, looking squarely at the opponent, your neck relaxed.
- At the same time as the last point, extend your relaxed left forearm towards the opponent, with your hand open but relaxed and your palm facing the opponent; there should be approximately a span's width between your arms.
- You should end with your left shoulder, knee and toes aligned on the same vertical line, your hilt and your right foot on the same vertical line, and your heels on the same line that goes between you and the opponent.

How to advance and retreat – In Italian rapier, you can advance and retreat in three main ways (I'll describe only the advance—for the retreat, invert the instructions starting with the opposite foot):

- With gathering or "chasing" steps, i.e., by bringing the left foot close to the right, then moving the right foot forward by the same distance, which makes you end in the same stance as when you were in guard.

- By bringing your right foot between a half and a whole shoe-length forward, then bringing your left foot forward by the same distance, which makes you end in the same stance as when you were in guard. This is the one I teach first, and the one that has given me the best pedagogical results.
- With passing steps, i.e., by bringing your left foot forward ahead of the right (toes still pointing left), then bringing the right foot forward ahead of the left by the same distance (toes still pointing at the opponent), which makes you end in the same stance as when you were in guard.

Inside line and outside line – These are the two main lines of offense in Italian rapier, and are used for attacks to the chest, face or head. Inside: when you and your opponent are in guard or execute an action and your sword is to the right of your opponent's, you both are to (or on) the inside. Outside: when you and your opponent are in guard or execute an action and your sword is to the left of your opponent's, you both are to (or on) the outside.

Low line and high line – These are the other two lines in Italian rapier. Low line: the line used for attacks to the flank (i.e., lower chest or torso) or leg. High line: when the opponent lowers his weapon into the low line and you execute an action to his chest, face or head, you are using the high line.

Lines in sword and dagger – The lines with sword and dagger are not defined as consistently. The most commonly-used lines are above the sword, between the weapons, above the dagger and below the dagger. The terms "inside" and "outside" are used more rarely, since there are two weapons (outside the sword would be different from outside the dagger, for instance).

Note: when Giganti tells you to advance on the side of the opponent's sword, he means to the outside of it.

The lunging thrust – From the guard, quickly extend your sword-arm straight towards the opponent, then violently bring your body forward with a simultaneous forward motion of the right foot. A lunging thrust to the inside ends with your hand in quarta; one to the outside, in seconda. Giganti's illustrations and signature explanation of this action (as well as the recovery) require no more words.

Gaining the opponent's sword – Gaining the opponent's sword means situating your weapon in such a way that he cannot perform an offensive action without changing lines by means of a cavazione (see "cavazione" on following page).

In Giganti, gaining the sword is always performed with the true edge—in this he does not admit the exceptions that other Masters sometimes advocate.[7] When you gain the opponent's sword to the inside, your hand is in terza-quarta, your blade crosses over the

---

7 When the false edge was used to gain the opponent's sword, it was mainly to the outside—examples include Masters such as Fabris and, most notably, Marcelli.

opponent's (forte on debole) and your sword-point is directed above the opponent's right shoulder. When you gain the opponent's sword to the outside, your hand is in seconda-terza, your blade crosses over the opponent's (forte on debole) and your sword point is directed above the opponent's left shoulder.

On whichever side you gain the opponent's sword, you are satisfying these four conditions:

1. The point of intersection of the blades is closer to your hilt than to his (forte on debole).
2. Your blade is above his.
3. Your sword crosses over his; and it remains in (or near) the opponent's presence, meaning pointed to (or not far from) the silhouette of his body or head.
4. If he attacks with a thrust without first changing lines with a cavazione, you will have in effect "pre-parried" his thrust.

Note: early 17th-century Masters such as Giganti advocate performing this action with little or no pressure against the opponent's blade.

The cavazione and half cavazione – A cavazione is a thrusting attack that is preceded by or incorporates a spiral motion around the opponent's weapon to free your sword while or after the opponent gains it. In other words, it is a thrusting attack with a line-change. Cavazioni can proceed inside to outside (and vice-versa) and high line to low line (and vice-versa). A half cavazione in Italian rapier is mainly one that starts from the inside or outside lines and ends on the low line.

As Giganti says, use the hand (i.e., the joint of the wrist) to perform this action, not the elbow or the whole arm. Cavazioni can be performed under or above the opponent's weapon—Giganti specifies when to use one or the other.

Which hand positions to use – Here is where Giganti's book departs from standard Italian rapier terminology, although he does not deviate from the physical way the actions are performed. Following is how you should keep your hand in Giganti—and in the greatest majority of Masters in the Italian tradition:

- When standing in guard, keep your hand in terza
- When gaining the opponent's sword or performing a simple parry to the inside, turn your hand in terza-quarta
- When gaining the opponent's sword or performing a simple parry to the outside, turn your hand in seconda-terza
- When performing a thrusting attack or counterattack to the inside, turn your hand in quarta
- When performing a thrusting attack or counterattack to the outside, turn your hand in seconda

Cuts – Cuts are employed quite often in Italian swordsmanship, with some Masters (like Alfieri) using them more than others. The three most useful cuts in Italian rapier are:

- The mandritto fendente, a descending true-edge cut you deliver from the right to the left, almost vertically, to the opponent's head
- The riverso fendente, a descending true-edge cut you deliver from the left to the right, almost vertically, to the opponent's head
- The riverso to the leg, an oblique true-edge cut you deliver from the left to the right to the opponent's right calf.

Cuts employ a simultaneous percussive and slicing motion involving the length of the debole, and they should be strong and smartly delivered. To the average rapier student, I recommend delivering them from the elbow; to stronger students, from the wrist.

Targets in Italian rapier – For the thrust, the main targets are the chest, the flank and the face. For the cut, they are the head and the limbs. Cuts to the body or thrusts to the limbs are consistently rare in 1500–1600 Italian swordsmanship. With sword and dagger, the shoulders also become targets for the thrust.

Measure – This is the distance between you and the opponent. In measure: a distance from which you can reach the opponent with a lunging thrust. Out of measure: a distance from which you cannot reach the opponent even with a lunging thrust. Within measure: a distance shorter than when you are in measure.

Tempo – Stripped of its illustrious philosophical pedigree,[8] a tempo (Italian for "time") is nothing but an opportune moment to strike the opponent according to the rules of the art, or at least to safely gain an advantage over him. Giganti is wonderfully concise on the subject in the chapter dedicated to tempo and measure, and I won't repeat what he says here. The only thing I can add is this: the more you stay with Giganti's advice on tempo, the better you will fare. Attacking out of tempo is the single most prominent bad habit I have observed in the Western martial arts community, as well as the easiest to cure with judicious drilling and a solid understanding of rapier theory (which is simple).

Full-intent actions and feints – A full-intent action is a simple attack designed to strike the opponent directly, without a feint. For instance, after gaining his sword, a full-intent action would be a straight thrust gliding along his blade (glide); or after he gains your sword, a full-intent action would be a cavazione. A feint is a compound attack whose first motion (the feint proper) is designed to provoke a parry, and whose subsequent motion (the cavazione) is designed to defeat the parry and to strike. As an attack, a feint cannot exist without a cavazione.

---

8 In the Renaissance, the notions of tempo were derived primarily from Aristotle's *Physics*: tempo (time) was defined as the measurement of motion between two instances of stillness, or of stillness between two motions.

The correct way to execute a feint is this: extend your arm and the sword-point smartly towards the target, as if performing the initial motion of a lunging thrust. As the opponent motions to parry, perform the cavazione and complete your lunging thrust on the new line.

Invitations – An invitation (called a "deceitful guard" by Giganti) is when you create a deliberate opening for the opponent to attack. When he does so, you defeat him with a well-planned counter. Every time you move your sword away from the ideal line that goes from your chest to the opponent's, you are de facto performing an invitation.

How to start an action – In Italian rapier generally, most actions are started in one of three ways:

- By gaining the opponent's sword, then
    - Defeating his cavazione or
    - Performing a full-intent thrust by gliding along his blade (glide) or
    - Performing a feint by glide
- By presenting the point in line so he gains or attempts to gain your sword, then
    - Performing a full-intent cavazione or
    - Performing a feint by cavazione
- By performing an invitation, then
    - Defeating his attack in various ways

Exceptions include taking the tempo from the opponent's motion, performing beats and other actions on the blade, performing feints without first gaining the opponent's blade, etc. However, you will notice that the above-mentioned three points cover the greatest majority of Giganti's repertoire; my advice, and Giganti's, is to get truly proficient in these basics.

I do not want this section to become a miniature rapier treatise of its own, since I only wish to present the very basics, and the concepts Giganti skips or does not describe in much depth. So, most other concepts and actions can be understood by reading Giganti's text. I have used footnotes to explain terms that appear throughout the book, so as to make it easier to follow the Master's words. I have also included a brief glossary at the end of the book, to explain in concise but clear words any technical terms used throughout the book.

Lastly, here are some additional resources where you can obtain more information or ask questions:

- The Freelance Academy Press Web site (www.freelanceacademypress.com)
- The Order of the Seven Hearts Web site (www.salvatorfabris.com)
- The Order of the Seven Hearts forum (www.salvatorfabris.com/forum)

- The Sword Forum International (www.swordforum.com)
- Guy Windsor's book on rapier *The Duellist's Companion*
- My translation of Salvator Fabris' 1606 rapier treatise *Scienza d' Arme*, which you can find under the title *The Art of Dueling*
- The foil section of Dr. William Gaugler's book *The Science of Fencing*, which although presenting a modern Classical system, is perhaps the clearest book in English that deals with a point weapon related to the rapier
- The many reputable historical-fencing symposia held worldwide, for instance (in the USA) WMAW, ISMAC, 4W, and others

And now, follow me into Giganti's *School, or Salle* and enjoy with me his superb rapier curriculum.

The School, or Salle

In which are represented various ways and means to defend and attack with single sword and sword and dagger; and whereby students may practice and become proficient in the discipline of arms

By Nicoletto Giganti of Venice

1606

The Guards and Counter-guards

There are several things you need to know if you want to become proficient in the art of arms. I will begin my lessons with the guards and counter-guards, also called postures and counter-postures of the sword. This is because when you are faced with some unexpected situation, this is the first thing you need to be familiar with to stand safely against the opponent.

As you will see in the illustrations, there are many points you must observe when you set yourself in guard. These are:

- Stand solidly on your feet, which are the base and the foundation of the whole body, in a measured stance, i.e., one that is preferably narrow rather than wide so that you have the capability to extend it
- Hold the sword and the dagger fast in your hands
- Keep the dagger sometimes high, sometimes low and sometimes extended
- Keep the sword sometimes high, sometimes low, sometimes to your inside and always ready to parry and strike, so that if the opponent attacks you with a thrust or a cut you can parry and counterattack in a single tempo
- Keep the body well-placed and at the ready, because lacking these two points, it will be easy for the opponent to unsettle you with a mandritto, a riverso, a thrust or other actions—which means that even if you parry his attack, you may still be vulnerable
- Point the dagger at the opponent's shoulder, so that you can use it to parry any attack he makes
- Always point your sword at the opponent's opening, so that when you attack, he will be hit

The whole artistry in our discipline consists of this: when you launch an attack, the opponent should receive a hit.

Furthermore, please note that every motion of the sword is a guard to the knowledgeable fencer, and all guards are useful to the experienced man; conversely, no motion is a guard to the ignorant, and no guard is effective for someone who does not know how to use it.

This discipline calls for knowledge and practice: when practiced, it becomes knowledge. Setting yourself in guard and showing the opponent an opening is an artful way to unsettle him and make him vulnerable; as is setting yourself in guard fully covered, so that you can advance on the opponent and strike him. This is why I say that every guard is useful to the knowledgeable and skilled fencer, while no guard is effective for someone who has no knowledge or skills. This will suffice as to guards.

Let's now discuss counter-guards. If you have any notion of this discipline, you will never set yourself in guard, but you will always attempt to be in a counter-guard. To set yourself against the opponent's guard, stand out of measure, with the sword and the dagger high, strong in your body-placement and with your stance firm and secure; then, examine the opponent's guard and slowly proceed to gain his sword by just about resting your blade over his, as if covering it. In this manner, he won't be able to perform an attack without first performing a cavazione.

Here's the reason for this action: as the opponent performs a cavazione, he executes two motions. The first motion (or tempo) is the cavazione itself; the second motion (or tempo) is the attack. While he performs the cavazione, you may attack him in many ways before he even has time to strike, as I will show in the illustrations.

If he changes guards by virtue of your counter-guard, follow him with your sword forward and the dagger extended, maintaining the advantage of the sword. By doing this, you can always attack him in the first tempo of his cavazione, and he can never perform an attack without doing so in two tempi, making it easy for you to defend.

And this will suffice about the guards and counter-guards.

Tempo and Measure

You can't truly say that you understand defense and offense if you only know how to stand in guard or in counter-guard; nor if you also know how you deliver a thrust, an imbroccata, a mandritto or a riverso; nor if you are also good at turning your hand, bearing your body, or maintaining the advantage over the opponent's blade. You can only make that claim if you have a command of tempo and measure.

Without the knowledge of these two concepts, you may parry or deliver an attack, but without really knowing how to do so; because in both parrying and delivering an attack, it is possible to make several mistakes and get into danger.

So, after speaking of the guards and counter-guards, I will discuss tempo and measure to give you a precise understanding of when to parry or execute an attack.

Measure is that distance from which you can reach the opponent with your sword. When you cannot, you are instead out of measure.

Tempo is recognized in the following ways. Suppose your opponent is in guard; stand in guard out of measure, gain his sword and observe what he does next.

- If he performs a cavazione, you can attack him while he does so, and this is a tempo
- If he changes guards, while he does so is a tempo
- If he delivers an attack, this is a tempo
- If he advances to come into measure, while he takes his step (and before he arrives in measure), this is a tempo
- If he delivers an attack, and you parry and counterattack in a single tempo, this too is a tempo
- If the opponent stands motionless in guard and waits, and you advance into measure and immediately deliver your attack into his opening, this is a tempo
- Every motion of the sword, dagger, foot or body (like changing guards) is a tempo

All these actions are tempi because they contain various intervals of time. While the opponent executes one of these motions, he must necessarily receive your hit because since he is moving, he cannot strike you at the same time. This theory explains how to defend and attack, as I will show in greater detail in the illustrations.

1 – Delivering a Lunging Thrust

How to Deliver the Thrust

After discussing the guards, counter-guards, measures and tempi, I need to show and explain how to carry your body while delivering a thrust and recovering. While studying this art, you must first learn how to carry your body and deliver lunging thrusts that are as long as the one you see in this illustration. The heart of the matter is the ability to deliver quick, long, strong lunging thrusts and immediately recover out of measure.

To deliver a lunging thrust, set yourself in a solid stance, better if a bit narrower rather than wide so that you may then extend your front foot forward. While delivering the thrust, extend the sword-arm and bend the knee as much as possible.

Here is the correct way to deliver this attack. After getting in guard, first extend the arm, then extend your body forward (in one tempo), so that the attack arrives on target before the opponent realizes it is coming. If you moved your body forward first, he would see it and use the tempo to parry and deliver a simultaneous counterattack.

Recover by moving the head back first, then the body and lastly the foot. If you recovered your foot first while your head and body remained forward, you would make yourself vulnerable.

To learn this art correctly, you first need to practice this thrust; once you know how to deliver it, the rest will be easy to learn, but not vice-versa.

Please be advised that I will often employ this method of delivering a thrust in my lessons, as the occasion will require, to make the lesson clearer. Let it not be said that I repeat myself unnecessarily.

Why I Begin with Single Sword

This is my first fencing book, and I will only discuss two weapons: the single sword and the sword and dagger. I will keep other weapons for future books that, God willing, I will soon have the opportunity to write. I decided to start with the sword since it is the most common and the most used among weapons; if you are skillful in handling it, you will also know how to employ nearly every other weapon.

And since carrying a dagger, targa or rotella is not common in every part of the world, and you would be therefore compelled by necessity to rely on your sword, I urge everyone to begin with the sword even though in actual combat you may have a dagger, targa or rotella at your disposal. Also, the dagger, targa or rotella may be accidentally dropped during combat; but if you can use the sword, you still would be able to defend yourself and strike the opponent with it. If you develop your skills with the single sword, you will be able to parry and deliver attacks as proficiently as if you had the sword and a dagger.

2 – *Gaining the opponent's sword to the inside (fencer on the left)*[9]

3 – *Gaining the opponent's sword to the outside (fencer on the left)*[10]

9 To further clarify this position, the two fencers are using the inside line, i.e., each is facing the opponent with his own blade to the right of the opponent's. The fencer on the left has gained the opponent's sword with his hand in quarta or terza-quarta.

10 To further clarify this position, the two fencers are using the outside line, i.e., each is facing the opponent with his own blade to the left of the opponent's. The fencer on the left has gained the opponent's sword with his hand in seconda or seconda-terza.

Guards, or Postures

In single sword, there are many guards and many counter-guards. In this first book, I only want to teach two types, which you may be able to use for every lesson here.

Before you perform an action, you must gain your opponent's sword out of measure, assuring yourself of his weapon by placing your blade over his so that he can only strike you by employing two tempi: one to perform the cavazione, one to deliver the attack. This is how you must proceed against all guards (high or low, depending on how your opponent is situated).

Again, your goal is to take away the opponent's ability and opportunity to strike you in a single tempo. To this effect, you must ensure that his blade is not pointed at your body so that he may not strike you with a sudden strong thrust.

So, gain his sword with yours, as you see in the illustration, so that the opponent does not have his point directed at your body and is therefore unable to hit you without a cavazione. Stand securely on your feet, your body steady and your arm extended and strong so that you may parry and counterattack—as shown in the illustration.

If your opponent was in a high or low guard and you failed to set yourself in this guard and to assure yourself of his sword, you would be in danger even against someone less knowledgeable and experienced than you. The action could easily end in a double-hit, or he could force you to parry or put you into obedience[11] by means of feints, cavazioni or other actions. Conversely, if you assure yourself of his sword as I have stated above, he will be unable to move or to perform any sort of action without you seeing it and being able to defend yourself.

The illustrations you see here show two guards with the swords extended, and two counter-guards with advantage over the opponent's sword; one is gaining the opponent's sword to the inside, the other to the outside (as the illustrations show and as I will say more of in the following lessons).

11 Obedience: an opponent goes to the obedience when he responds to your action with the action (typically a parry) that you intended to provoke. In this sense, he is obeying you.

4 – Strike in the tempo of the opponent's cavazione, after gaining his sword to the inside

Explanation of the Strike in Tempo

This illustration teaches you how to strike your opponent in the tempo of his cavazione. Gain your opponent's sword from out of measure, placing your blade over his to the inside (just as shown by the fencer in the first illustration of the guards), so that the opponent cannot attack you without a cavazione. So, in the very tempo in which he performs it to attack you, push your sword forward turning your hand at the same time, and strike him in the face as shown in the illustration.

If you were to first parry and then strike, the action would not succeed because the opponent would have time to parry and to place you in danger. But if you move forward at once in the tempo of his cavazione and turn your hand (which is the parry), the opponent will find it difficult to defend. After doing this (and whether the opponent has received your hit or not), safely recover out of measure with your sword over the opponent's, never relinquishing the advantage over his blade.

Lastly, if the opponent does not perform the cavazione, advance into measure while maintaining the advantage of the sword, and immediately attack his opening with a thrust; then, recover out of measure placing your blade lightly over his.

5 – *Strike in the tempo of the opponent's cavazione, after gaining his sword to the outside*

The Correct Way to Gain the Opponent's Sword and Strike Him while He Performs a Cavazione

This illustration teaches you that if the opponent is in guard to the outside (with his sword high or low), gain his blade to the outside from out of measure, barely resting your blade over his and standing over a solid stance that is neither too wide nor too narrow. Keep your sword ready to parry and counterattack and keep your eye alert—as you see in the second illustration of the guards and counter-guards.

If you set yourself as I have just described, the opponent will not be able to attack you with a thrust without first performing a cavazione; if he does so, turn your hand and, in the same tempo, deliver your thrust as shown in the illustration. Then, recover out of measure immediately (and in the same tempo), resting your blade over his. If he performs another cavazione, push another thrust in the same way, turning the hand and then again recovering out of measure. So, you may turn your hand and deliver a thrust as many times as he performs a cavazione.

To be good at this type of play, you need much practice, because it is from this that you learn to parry and strike with great agility and speed.

Please observe that you should always remain steady with your body, and that you should parry with the forte of the sword; for if the opponent's attack is strong, your strong defense will unsettle him, enabling you to hit him where he is open. This is the first lesson you should learn with the single sword, since it is from this lesson that all the others in this book originate. And if you know how to do this in tempo, you will know how to parry all the cuts and all the full-intent thrusts[12] that may be aimed at your head (as you will see in the lessons that follow).

The Correct Way to Perform a Cavazione

The two fencers I have just illustrated above display how to strike the opponent while he performs a cavazione. Since I want the elements in my lessons to be perfectly clear, I will now discuss the correct way for you to perform a cavazione.

Proceed to gain your opponent's sword while he is situated in whatever guard, and deliver a thrusting attack to his opening. If the opponent is as knowledgeable as you, your swords will always be in parity,[13] and in that case, perform a cavazione under his hilt while quickly turning your hand and, in the same tempo, deliver your thrust to his opening. This is the correct and safe way to perform a cavazione and striking in one tempo.

If you were to perform the cavazione without turning your hand, you would give your opponent a tempo and an opportunity to strike you, as you will easily see for yourself while practicing.

If the opponent parries, perform another cavazione as described, always ensuring you turn your hand. You will therefore perform as many cavazioni as the opponent does parries—but always making sure you do so in the manner I explained, which is perfectly safe—and follow with a thrust in the same tempo as the cavazione.

A cavazione as I have described is just as useful as parrying as I have discussed in the previous illustration, and this is the most important set of skills you should develop as you learn the single sword. This is why I urge you to practice these two techniques assiduously; this way, if you are in measure against your opponent and he gives you a tempo to perform a cavazione, you can do so quickly and accurately; likewise, as you are presented with a tempo in which you must parry, you can also do so with exactness.

---

12 A full-intent thrust (*punta risoluta*) is a thrust not performed as a feint, but with the explicit intention of hitting the opponent. It stands in contrast with the feinted thrust.

13 Parity of swords (*parita' di spada*) occurs when, in the course of an action, neither of the two opposing swords has a mechanical advantage over the other.

6 – Contracavazione against the opponent's cavazione, after gaining his sword to the inside

The Contracavazione to the Inside

This illustration shows and explains another way to defend yourself and strike the opponent—with a contracavazione. Here is how this action is performed.

Gain your opponent's sword so that he will require a cavazione if he wishes to attack; as he performs the cavazione, perform one of your own, so that your two swords will end up on the side where you started, with you having the advantage of the sword. In the same tempo as your cavazione, deliver a thrust to his opening, turning your hand well towards the inside and keeping your arm extended (so that if he attacks you, his body will meet your point).

After delivering this thrust, recover out of measure.

7 – Contracavazione against the opponent's cavazione, after gaining his sword to the outside

The Contracavazione to the Outside

Striking with a contracavazione to the outside is similar to the same action done to the inside. The only difference is as follows.

If the opponent advances against you, employ the counter-guard and gain his blade to the outside to provoke a cavazione. As he performs it, execute a cavazione in the same tempo, circling your point under his and turning your hand; then, with the true edge placed over his blade, glide along his steel with your arm well extended, your body limber and your step extended as shown in the illustration. By doing all this, you will strike your opponent without him even realizing it.

Be advised that if the opponent's attack is forceful, you will need to keep your body back as you perform the cavazione, to prevent his point from reaching and striking you. In this case, the opponent will be unsettled by the very violence of his own thrust and will come and meet your point. You will then have the advantage, and you will be able to strike him where you please.

Also, please always bear in mind to keep your sword out of your presence,[14] so as to remain safe.

14 Giganti is referring to the concept of opposition, although the specific fencing term does not appear until at least a century later. In layman's terms, this means situating your hilt and forte so as to push or exclude the opponent's point from your silhouette ("out of your presence") while you attack or counterattack. Opposition is effected by forming an obtuse angle between the sword-arm and the blade, and it is the main mechanical way to avoid receiving a hit while delivering an attack.

8 – Feint by cavazione inside-outside, and cavazione to the inside

Feints—Explanation. The Feint of Cavazione from the Hand

Since there are several offensive actions, there will be several lessons in this book. However, do not expect me to list every single offensive action that is possible in our discipline: as their number is limitless, this book would end up being too long and wearisome to the reader. For this reason, I will only explain the actions that I consider more striking, artistic and useful. And among the artful ways to strike the opponent, feints are in my opinion distinctly superior to all others.

Feinting means motioning to do one thing and doing another. Feints can be performed in different ways, which I will now describe.

Set yourself in guard to the inside, with the sword in front of you and your arm well extended, so as to provoke the opponent to gain your sword. As the opponent steps into measure, assess whether he intends to strike you with a firm-footed attack[15] or with a pass; you will know this when you perform your cavazione. So, perform your cavazione from the hand and feint a thrust to his face; however, feint your thrust wide, to ensure that the opponent's steel won't meet yours.

If he does not parry, push your thrust home, and you will hit him for sure. If he parries, perform an additional cavazione and strike him as pictured in this illustration, where the opponent has incautiously run against his adversary's point.

---

15 Firm-footed attack (*ferita a pie' fermo*): an attack with footwork other than a pass, i.e., a lunging attack or an attack without a motion of either foot.

Be sure not to let the opponent's blade touch yours as you perform your second cavazione, otherwise your action will fail. Also, keep your head and body a little withdrawn, so you can safely judge what the opponent has in mind; if he attacks without you using this precaution, the action would result in a double hit. Lastly, be sure to glide with your true edge against the edge of the opponent's steel, turning your hand upward as you contact his debole; then, after your thrust or feinted thrust, recover out of measure, assuring yourself of the opponent's weapon, as I have previously described.

In summary, this is how a feint is performed:

- First, present your point to the opponent's face or chest, extending your arm (but not your step)
- If the opponent parries, perform a cavazione in the same tempo and push your thrust home accompanied with the extension of your foot, and you will hit him for sure
- If he does not parry your feint, extend your step and push your thrust home

This is how you strike with a feint.

Note: the following two illustrations may seem to be the same but they are not, since they arise from different feinting actions although ending in the same strikes. I may have just used one illustration to show and explain various feinting actions; however, I opted for showing two, since they are the result of two distinctly different actions (which I will make clear in the text accompanying them).

9 – Feint by cavazione outside-inside, [half] cavazione to the low line, strike to the chest

How to Strike to the Chest with Single Sword—from the Measure and Parity of Swords

This illustration shows an artful manner to strike the opponent in the chest while assuring yourself of his weapon so that he may not attack you as you perform your pass. Following is the description of this action.

Set yourself in guard with your sword extended and to the outside; if the opponent comes to gain your sword, let him do so until he steps into measure. As soon as he is in measure, perform a cavazione to the inside and present your point to his face: if he does not parry, push your thrust home gliding with your true edge against the edge of his sword, turning your hand and bringing your body somewhat to the side.

If he instead parries and counterattacks as you perform the cavazione, refrain from thrusting, but keep your point a bit wide of his; and as he attempts the parry and counterattack, perform another cavazione under his hilt and keep your point directed at the opponent's chest. In this manner, you will certainly be able to strike him in the chest, bringing your sword well forward as depicted.

Please make sure your two cavazioni are executed in the same tempo without stopping the motion of your point, or else the opponent's steel may meet it. As he attempts to parry, pass to the outside all the way to the opponent's body with your hand on his hilt. This pass takes it out of his power to strike you while enabling you to hit him in any way you please.

10 – Feint to the inside, low-line strike to the chest with a left-foot pass

The Pass with Feint from out of Measure

This is an artful way to pass against the opponent without him realizing it, and it is a momentous action because of the show it makes, as you can see in the illustration. It consists of passing with a feint, and proceeding to strike the opponent. Here is how it is performed.

Observe in which guard the opponent stands; as soon as he is set in his guard, advance against him with your sword pointed at his face. As soon as you are almost in measure (and he is waiting for you motionless), deliver a powerful thrust towards his face, as shown in illustration… If he does not parry with sufficient strength, this action will end with the strike shown in illustration…[16] and you will not need to perform any feints. But if he does, your two blades will end in a position of equal strength, so immediately recover out of measure into your initial guard.

Then, advance again and when you are almost in measure, feint a similar thrust to his face; as he attempts the parry, use your hand to perform a cavazione with your point under his hilt , making sure to keep his point out of your presence. In the same tempo, pass while gliding with your sword above his hilt, immediately placing your left hand on his hilt. The action of the left hand ensures that he won't strike you with a riverso to the face. By doing all this, you will hit him for sure, without him even realizing what you are doing.

16 Giganti mistakenly omits the number of the plates to which he refers the reader. However, they would be plates showing a strike to the face from the inside, such as in illustrations 6 and 8.

Afterwards, recover by jumping[17] out of measure, and gain the opponent's sword as described. Then, after beating his sword, you can again strike him with two or three full-intent thrusts that are impossible to parry.

The Pass with Feint above the Opponent's Point

This is another type of cavazione and feint, which is not seen very often. This too will end in a position similar to that of the last two illustrations. Here is how this action is performed.

Set yourself in guard to the outside, with the arm extended, so as to let the opponent gain your blade as described. As he arrives in measure, perform a cavazione above the point of his sword. If he does not parry, push a strong, full-intent thrust as I have described elsewhere (which won't require any feints). If he parries, do not stop the motion of your sword, but avoid the opponent's hilt and pass as described in the previous illustration. After striking the opponent in the chest, recover as discussed.[18]

---

17 Giganti uses the verb *saltare*. By this, he could mean a quick retreat or an actual jump backward with both feet, a type of footwork sometimes encountered in historical Italian swordsmanship, especially in the 16th century.

18 This seems to be the action shown in illustration 10, since it does not entail a glide above the opponent's sword, but rather a hit to the low line while the opponent parries high.

11 – Strike to the face with a pass

The Feint to the Face from out of Measure

This action only differs from the other feint in the fact that in the former the cavazione ends under the opponent's blade, while in this it ends above—so as to strike him in the face. If this action is parried by the opponent, it turns into a feint; if not, it becomes a full-intent thrust. As far as everything else, please observe the same rules about guard, measures and distances. Likewise, carry your body and sword as illustrated, and once you have delivered your thrust, recover out of measure.

The important thing is that you perform the feint in a natural manner, so that the opponent cannot distinguish it from a full-intent thrust. Here is an example of how it is done.

First, perform a cavazione above his blade to the high outside, threatening his face; then, as you perform a cavazione under the opponent's hilt to hit him to the inside, make sure that your action ends with your point to his face or chest. This is the kind of natural feint I mean; be careful never to perform a feint unless the opponent attempts to parry your full-intent thrust—otherwise you will incur the danger of a double hit.[19]

---

19 The illustration shows a similar example, but starting from the outside. To arrive at the situation illustrated, first, perform a cavazione above his blade to the high inside; as he attempts the defense, perform an additional cavazione to the high outside, striking him in the face above his blade as depicted.

12 – Thrust in tempo against a mandritto

The Correct Way to Deliver a Thrust while the Opponent Attacks You with a Cut

This illustration shows how to use tempo to deliver a thrust to the opponent's face as he attacks you with a cut to the head. As he raises his sword, you can push your thrust while his weapon is lifted and before it reaches you. Here is how this action is performed.

Set yourself in whichever guard you please and advance against your opponent. If once in measure, the opponent attacks you with a cut to the head, use the tempo of his lifting his weapon, push forward and deliver a thrust to his face. Without a doubt, you will hit him as shown in the illustration, i.e., while his sword is in the air.

As you deliver your attack, turn your hand upward, with the true edge also upward and your arm high and extended, ensuring that your hilt covers your head. This way, you will be well covered and the opponent's sword won't be able to reach you as it comes down.

This thrust needs to be quick, or else the opponent may parry it and could strike you. And after you deliver it, quickly recover out of measure, assuring yourself of the opponent's weapon with yours.

In this, my first book, I decided not to include the many ways in which to parry cuts. I have discussed this one, however, since it is the most useful and the easiest in which to learn to recognize and employ the tempo (which you need to do in any case).

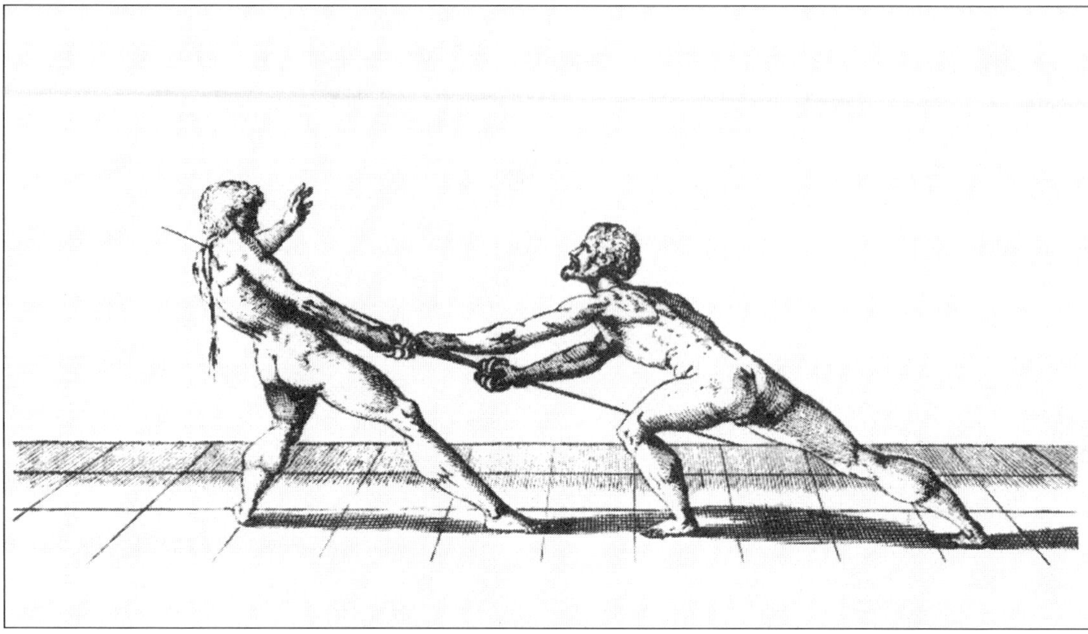

13 – A strike using both hands to fortify the sword

The Correct Way to Deliver a Sure Strike Using Both Hands

This illustration shows how to deliver a sure strike, since it is impossible to parry. It can be performed in two ways.

The first way is as follows. Find the opportunity to be to the outside without either of you having the advantage of the sword. Present your point to the opponent's face. If the opponent does not perform a strong parry, you may strike him in the face, as shown in the fourth illustration. Conversely, if he executes a good, strong parry, pass with the left foot placing your left hand on your sword and pressing down smartly with both hands. As you do this, direct your point to the opponent's chest and lower your hilt as you see in the illustration. Be sure to perform all this in a single tempo.

The second way is as follows. Set yourself in guard as described just above, but to the inside. Perform a cavazione to the outside, as if to strike; at the same time, place your left hand on your sword and, using the strength of both hands, beat the opponent's steel with yours. As his weapon is beaten wide, quickly pass forward with your left foot (as depicted). Be sure to perform all this in a single tempo—that is, the cavazione, the placing of your left hand on your sword, the beat and the left-foot pass. Conversely, you may fail and be in danger, as would happen especially against a skilled man who can perform fast and accurate cavazioni. So be sure to do all this quickly and suddenly.

14 – How to defend against a cut to the leg

The Correct Way to Defend against a Mandritto or a Riverso to the Leg

This lesson deals with the mandritto or riverso to the leg; I will not say any more about how to defend and counterattack in a single tempo—actually, the opponent will come and stick himself on your point.

If the opponent attacks you with a mandritto or riverso, he must extend his right foot and project his body and head forward. As he does this, withdraw your right leg and deliver a thrust to his face in the same tempo; this will cause the opponent to stick himself on your point, without being able to defend or to hit you. Then, recover out of measure, as I have often explained.

This lesson is quite artful, so make sure you understand it so you can use it when called for in a situation similar to that depicted here.

15 – The inquartata

The Inquartata or Void

The inquartata (or void) is necessary to refine body control. This action is not ordinarily used in schools, but it's used by the French to exercise the body. Actually, there are several voiding actions (or inquartate); but in this book, I chose to only show three as the safest and the more showy—as you can see from the image.

First inquartata – Set yourself in guard to the inside, with the right foot forward, the sword and the arm extended, with your blade pointing to the opponent's face. Let the opponent advance and gain your sword; when he has almost reached the measure, feint with a cavazione (a little wide); use the tempo of the opponent's parry to perform a cavazione to the inside, close to his edge, so that you will strike him right at the end of the cavazione. (If you were to perform the cavazione first and then strike, it would become a two-tempi action and you might place yourself in danger.)

As you do this, turn your body and shoulder by performing an oblique step with your left foot, and you will strike the opponent in the face or chest as depicted, without him realizing your design. Keep your arm taut, and use your hilt to protect yourself and to keep the opponent's steel away from you. Look into the opponent's face, and make sure you do not turn yours as you perform this action (as some do), or else you won't be able to see what you are doing and you would be in danger.

Right afterwards, recover back out of measure with your sword over his, as I have described other times.

Second inquartata – This inquartata only differs from the one just described in the strike, which stays close to the opponent's edge but ends under the opponent's pommel, with your arm and hand lifted (as depicted). After performing this void, stop and do not proceed against the opponent's body so as to avoid coming to grips, which may place you in danger as you may not be able to recover out of measure and be safe.

This second inquartata is extremely difficult to parry—I would say impossible—when it is done with exactness.

Third inquartata – The third inquartata is the most showy and the safest. Here is how it is performed. Set yourself in guard like in the other two, with your sword to the inside, with your arm extended and firm. As the opponent advances and gains your blade, wait until he is in measure; then, perform a cavazione and turn your hand. If he does not parry, push your thrust home to his face and you will have performed the action shown in the illustration,[20] nor will you need to do anything else.

If he does, your swords will be in parity. Press with your blade against his, so he will press back. As you feel his pressure, perform the cavazione and the inquartata, and strike him in the chest under his pommel, which he will not see. After ending in the position shown in the illustration, recover out of measure assuring yourself of his sword as in the other lessons.

An Artful Way to Strike the Opponent in the Chest after Pressing against Each Other's Blades

The previous lessons taught you how to perform an inquartata after pressing against each other's blades to the outside—striking to the inside. In this one, we will briefly see how to do so to the outside after pressing against each other's blades to the inside.

As your blades meet, press smartly against his with your edge, keeping your point aimed at his face and ensuring that your forte is above his blade. If he is weaker than you, he will be unable to parry your thrust to his face or chest. If he is not, as soon as you feel his pressure, perform a cavazione under his hilt (and his sword will fall towards the ground), and he will receive a thrust that is impossible to parry. In the same tempo, pass forward, without any danger, and place your left hand to his hilt. You may then strike him with three or four thrusts, as he will be unable to defend against them. Then, recover out of measure, assuring yourself of his sword as described.

20 Giganti does not say which, but it is quite likely the one showing how to perform a cavazione correctly—i.e., a strike in seconda to the outside.

How to Play Single Sword against Single Sword, with Full-intent Thrusts

There are many who, in the salle, attack the opponent with full intent and deliver thrusts, imbroccate and cuts without any respect to tempo, but always throwing blows with fury and vehemence. This is the kind of play that will unsettle every good fencer, which is why it is important to know what to do against it.

Place yourself out of measure in a defensive counter-guard, over a rather narrow stance. As the opponent delivers a thrust, imbroccata or cut (or any other attack), beat his blade with your forte and immediately follow with a thrust to his face or chest—with the extension of the right foot.

Then, recover your foot back to where it was before, assuring yourself of his sword by placing your blade over his: by doing this, he will be unable to attack you without performing a cavazione. If he performs it, turn your hand to the outside, beat his blade again and perform the same action. And if he tries another cavazione, do the same again.

This lesson is more useful than pretty. You will be making two tempi (the first is the parry, the other the strike), which you should be able to do before the opponent makes a single one. The explanation above will suffice as to how they are executed.

16 – Parry and low-line counterthrust to the chest

How to Parry Thrusts to the Chest with Single Sword

This illustration shows you a safe way to parry thrusts to your chest and to deliver a counterthrust to the opponent's. This can be done in different ways; some pass from out of measure, others start in measure and others yet get inside the measure. If you have a good notion of tempo and are proficient at parrying like my illustration teaches you, you will be able to defend in any case.

Suppose you and the opponent are facing each other without any of you having the advantage of the blade and he passes to attack you with a thrust to the chest. In that same tempo, follow his blade with yours, lower your point by lifting your hand and parry. Pass with your left foot towards the opponent's right, removing your body from the threat of his point, and hit him in the chest while placing your left hand on his hilt. After delivering this thrust, perform a cavazione[21] as described before and recover out of measure.

21 From the low to the high line.

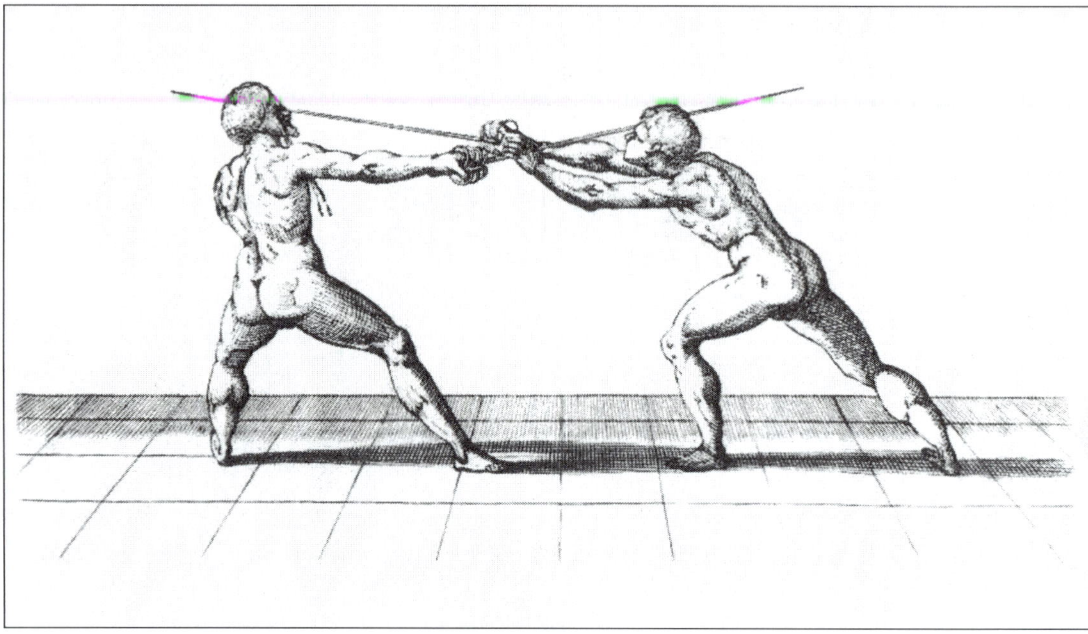

17 – Strike to the inside with a turn of the hand (yield) to foil the opponent's parry

The Thrust to the Face, Turning the Hand

This illustration shows a splendid way to strike your opponent in the face. The most important factor is to seize the occasion when neither of you has the advantage of the sword. Make the opponent parry by feinting with a cavazione; in the same tempo, turn your hand, place your left hand against his hilt and pass while delivering a thrust to his face (as shown). If you perform this action correctly, it will be impossible for him to parry.

After the attack, you can move forward with your left hand on his hilt, and after performing a cavazione, you can deliver two or three additional thrusts where you wish. Then, recover out of measure with your blade above his, as explained elsewhere.

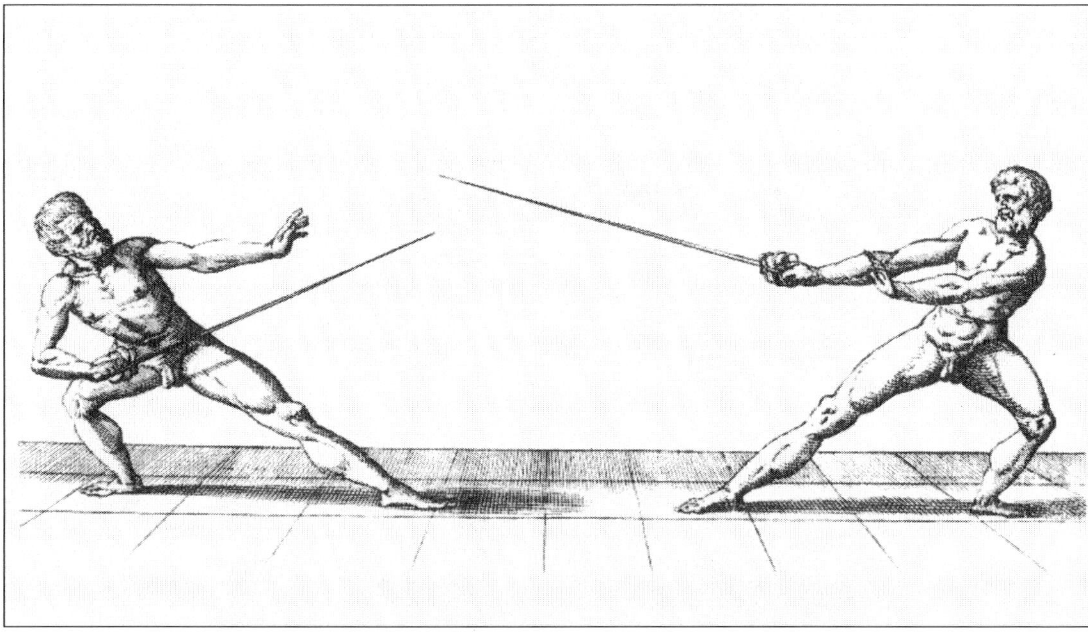

18 – Counterattack with a cavazione from out of measure (initial position: fencer on the right to execute the cavazione and counterattack)

19 – Counterattack with a cavazione from out of measure

Counterattack with a Cavazione from out of Measure

This is a counterattack with cavazione[22] from out of measure against an opponent who, from a left-foot-forward guard, attacks with a pass while turning his hand strongly to the inside.[23] The illustrations show both the initial positions and the action.

The following should help you understand the action better. When the opponent is situated in a left-foot-forward guard and moves forward to gain your sword, make sure you are in a similar guard as that illustrated, giving him an opening to attack your chest. A good opponent will quickly pass forward with his right foot and strongly turn his hand to the inside to shield himself from your blade.

In that same tempo, perform a cavazione under his hilt, lower your body as illustrated and strike him in the face before he finishes his attack—actually, even before his right foot hits the ground. He will be unable to parry this action.

This action requires you practicing the positions shown in these two illustrations.

---

22 Giganti uses the term *contracavazione*.

23 Giganti uses the term *passare d'inquartata*.

20 – Strike in the face with single sword against sword and dagger

How to Use Single Sword against Sword and Dagger

This illustration shows you how to defend against and strike an opponent armed with the sword and dagger when you have only your sword.

Stand in guard over a stance that is not too wide, the body back and the sword straight forward, ready to defend and strike when the tempo calls for it. Do not strike first, since against a good opponent you run the risk of him parrying your attack with his dagger while being unable to defend against his strike.

Instead, stand in guard as I have just described, ready to parry, and show a certain fear of him, so that he may attack you without taking the necessary precautions. As he launches his attack, parry strongly with your forte and strike him in the face. Since his attack will be long and strong, his dagger will likely offer the opening. As soon as you have completed your attack, recover out of measure, keeping your sword over his as described many times.

You can use this action as many times as he attacks you. However, be mindful not to direct your thrust to his chest, since this will not be as safe. Armed with sword and dagger, the opponent will be very much emboldened by seeing you holding only the sword; so, he will be likely to come forward and attack you rather carelessly. But if you stand in a good guard and are alert, you will be able to thwart his attack with a strong, positive parry, to deliver a thrust to his face and to safely recover out of measure with your sword above his.

If the opponent performs a cavazione to the inside, simply turn your hand, parry and deliver a strong counterattack as described. If you perceive that he wants to throw himself against your body, pull back and strike him in the tempo of his forward motion.

If you gain his sword while in guard and perceive that the opponent may first parry with the dagger, then deliver a riposte, use the tempo of his lowering his dagger for the parry to perform a cavazione above his dagger (as described in plate [...][24]), then immediately recover out of measure with your sword above his.

If he stands in his guard and does not attack, do not attack him unless he gives you a tempo—otherwise he may deceive you as we said when we discussed tempo and measure.

Lastly, if he stands in guard and waits (out of real or simulated hesitation), keep yourself out of measure with your sword above his, and wait to parry and strike safely, as the occasion requires.

24 Here too, Giganti mistakenly omits the plate number.

21 – Parry and counterattack against a thrust to the face

How to Parry a Thrust to the Face in Sword and Dagger

To perform the action illustrated here, you need to set yourself in guard in the manner already described, i.e., in a solid stance that is neither too narrow nor too wide, with both weapons ready so you can parry and strike as the occasion presents itself. Keep your dagger guarding the opponent's sword. If he attacks you with a thrust to the face, parry with the edge of the dagger and, in the same tempo, strike him with a thrust in the right armpit. Performing your action in one tempo will make it difficult for the opponent to parry.

To make this action succeed, you must not only understand the theory behind it, but also have the necessary agility to put theory into practice.

There are many things you need to mind at the same time. Start from a strong guard, with the right foot forward and the left foot steadily supporting the whole body. When the occasion arrives, be ready to quickly advance or retreat while keeping the point of your sword well directed at the opponent's face or chest and the dagger high, depending on the position of the opponent's sword. Also, mind to lean back with your body rather than forward, to keep your eye lively and attentive, and your heart valiant and free from any worry from the opponent.

And if you are in this guard and the opponent attacks you with a thrust or cut, parry with the edge of your dagger and execute the action depicted here. Make sure to parry crisply, holding your head and body slightly back; and while you parry his attack, deliver a strong counterattack in the same tempo. If you first parry and then deliver the attack, the action would not succeed, since the opponent has the time to withdraw his arms and body, parry, and place you in danger. This is why parrying and counterattacking in the same tempo enables you to deliver your thrust under the edge of the opponent's sword while he is still going forward. Do this with agility and in tempo, and it will be very difficult for him to defend himself.

Be advised to keep your left foot in place before delivering your counterattack, so that you can then immediately recover out of measure.

To recover correctly after delivering your thrust, first withdraw your head and body followed by your leg. If you withdraw your leg first, your head would remain forward and your whole body would be in danger and unable to escape out of measure. Remember that delivering a strong and deep attack is for naught if you can't recover correctly afterwards.

To perform the action shown in the picture, you need to gain enough experience that as soon as you perceive that the opponent is about to attack, you are ready to counterattack in the same tempo, confident that although he moves first, you strike first.

22 – Parry and counterattack against a thrust to the left flank

How to Correctly Parry a Thrust to the Left Flank

Start this action from the same position as for the previous one. Keep your dagger guarding the opponent's sword, and in the tempo of his attack to your left flank, parry with the edge of the dagger and strike him in the right shoulder. Do this in one tempo, and better yet, try to make your thrust quicker than his.

Stay alert with your eyes and mind, solid and tight with your body, and as soon as he intends to deliver his thrust, parry while pushing a thrust to his flank in the same tempo. He will be unable to parry, since your thrust will arrive as he is coming forward, just as you see in the illustration.

After your thrust, recover out of measure as described in the first action of sword and dagger.

23 – Parry and counterattack against a thrust to the right flank

How to Correctly Parry a Thrust to the Right Flank in Sword and Dagger

If you were in the guard I have described[25] and the opponent advanced on you with his sword low to attack your right flank, lift the sword arm and stay in the third guard[26] to deliver an imbroccata[27] with the point of your sword to the opponent's face or chest.

Keep your dagger low, and your arm guarding the opponent's sword. As the opponent begins his thrust, parry and deliver the imbroccata to his right shoulder all in one tempo, as you see in the illustration. Even better, as soon as you see that the opponent intends to attack, launch your thrust and you will strike him even more easily. After your thrust or imbroccata, recover out of measure.

These are the four ways to strike and parry with a stoccata or imbroccata. They all share the same nature, which is to parry and counterattack in a single tempo. As far as the feet, be always sure to advance your right foot as you deliver your attack, keeping your left foot steadily on the ground. At first, keeping the left foot this way may seem difficult, but it will get easier with practice.

---

25 In the first lesson of sword and dagger.

26 Giganti means the third guard he describes, i.e., the one with the opening between the weapons. Not to be confused with the traditional third guard or terza guardia, a nomenclature that Giganti does not follow.

27 Strong thrust with hand in prima.

24 – Parry and counterattack against a thrust to the face

How to Parry a Thrust to the Face in Sword and Dagger

This action requires your starting in the same guard I have described before. As the opponent delivers his attack to your face, parry with the edge of the dagger, and push a thrust to his flank in a single tempo.

As the opponent points his sword towards your face, be sure to keep your dagger wide, giving him an opening to deliver his attack. When he attacks, parry with the dagger, turn your head so that it is safe from his blade and, in the same tempo as the parry, push your thrust to his flank, which will be open and the nearest target.

Afterwards, recover as described.

25 – Parry and counterattack against a cut to the head

How to Parry a Cut to the Head in Sword and Dagger

This illustration teaches you how to parry a cut to the head with your dagger. Begin in the same guard as for the first lesson; if the opponent attacks you with a cut to the head, meet his blow with the edge of your dagger while in the same tempo delivering a thrust to his face accompanied by an extension of the front foot. Do these three things simultaneously, and you will have performed the action in the picture.

Against a powerful cut, it would be even better to do something to weaken the opponent's attack so that it only has half its strength. To do this, deliver your thrust to his face just as he lifts his sword in preparation for the cut; this will cause him to draw his head back and close his eyes, making his cut weaker. But this action requires several things—i.e., being fearless before the opponent and his sword; knowing how to parry with the dagger; knowing how to deliver a good, long thrust; and being careful not to parry with the flat of the dagger. The latter is because a strong cut parried that way would cause you to drop your weapon, and your head would get hit by the opponent's sword, while parrying with the edge and with a straight arm does not expose you to the same danger.

After delivering your thrust, recover out of measure as often described.

26 – Parry and counterattack against a riverso

How to Parry a Riverso with the Dagger

Here you'll learn how to parry a riverso to the face with your dagger. Start in the guard of the first lesson, with your dagger held firmly and high. As you see the riverso coming at you, meet it with the edge of the dagger, and in the same tempo extend your right foot and deliver a thrust to the opponent's flank, which will be open, and you will have performed the action shown in the illustration.

The previous six illustrations all have one thing in common: parrying the opponent's attack and striking him is done in the same tempo. If you were to do one first, then the other, you wouldn't be performing the same action—an action that requires practice and proficiency.

After delivering the thrust, recover out of measure.

Be advised that these six lessons are both the finest and the most important in fencing. Remember to hold your dagger firmly in your hand, and that as soon as you see the opponent's sword coming towards you with a thrust or a cut, meet it with the dagger while striking him where he is open in the same tempo.

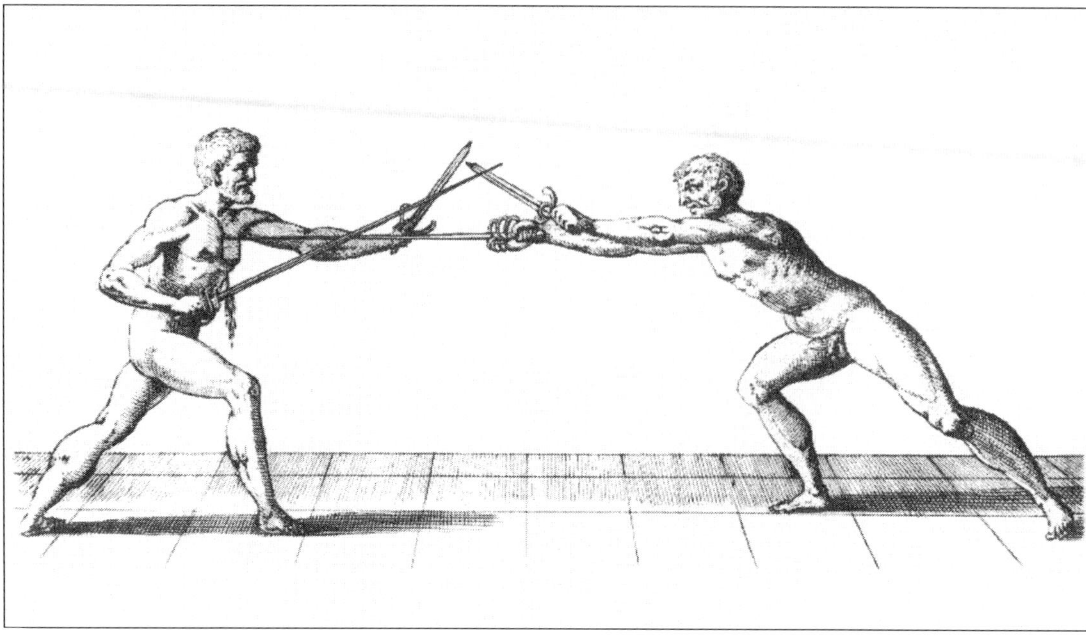

27 – Full-intent thrust to the chest

Thrust to the Chest in Sword and Dagger

The first thing you need to know if you want to learn how to fence is advancing on the opponent, striking him with a thrust and recovering in guard out of measure. To do this, you need to know the counter-guards and how to deliver a thrust where the opponent's openings are.

If his chest presents even a slight opening, advance slowly on him with your sword low, the point directed at his chest and the dagger guarding his sword. As soon as you are in measure, launch the attack to his chest by first extending your sword, then your body—and he won't even see it coming. If you instead extended first the body than the sword, your opponent would see the attack and may be able to defend himself and strike you in the same tempo, which would spell danger.

Right after your attack, recover back out of measure, with your weapons ready to parry and strike, since after receiving the hit, the opponent may attempt a last-ditch thrusting or cutting attack. So be ready to parry and strike in one tempo, as you have learned in the first six illustrations. But the importance of this illustration is mainly to teach you that after the attack, you should know how to recover out of measure; and that, to do so, you need to first recover your head, then your body and your leg. Starting the recovery with your leg would either put you in danger of falling or make you vulnerable to the opponent, since your head would still be forward. So make sure this is one of the main things you learn.

28 – *Full-intent thrust in the tempo of the opponent's motion*

Delivering a Thrust while the Opponent Moves

Understanding measure and tempo is the foundation of fencing, which is the subject of this action. As soon as you grip your sword and go against the opponent, advance towards him with an alert eye and with the weapons ready to parry and strike. This is the moment to assess whether the opponent wants to be the attacker or the defender. If you perceive that he wants to attack, give him a tempo to do so, and use his tempo to parry and strike him as you've seen above.

But if he shows himself to be timid and stands in guard waiting for you, advance against him on the side where he is open and, as you get into measure, keep your dagger forward guarding his sword, and then push your sword-point, then your body, then your foot forward for the attack. Keep your dagger always guarding his sword; this way, if he uses the tempo to attack you, you can still parry and avoid a double hit. After your attack, recover out of measure as described.

As you advance against the opponent, he must do one of these three things: he'll either attack, stand still waiting to parry, or move (to either side) to retreat out of measure. If he attacks or stands still to parry, you need to act as described in this lesson. If he moves or retreats on either side (or any other way), you should deliver a quick and strong thrust while his foot is lifted. While he moves, he will be unable to strike you in the tempo of your attack.

Afterwards, recover out of measure as described.

29 – *Full-intent thrust above the dagger*

Thrust above the Dagger

If the opponent keeps his dagger low, you need to proceed as you see in this illustration. Advance against him to the side of the dagger and, as you enter into measure, push your sword, then your body forward for the attack, while keeping your hand high as you see in the picture. Then, recover as described.

It is very difficult to defend yourself against those who are proficient in pushing first the sword, then the body for the attack and are quick to recover as we have described—and against those who can advance against the opponent in the right tempo, and who, once in measure, attack the opponent's openings. This is because the sword and dagger can't quite cover a man, and they necessarily leave some opening where he can be made vulnerable. Always advance on the side of the opponent's openings.

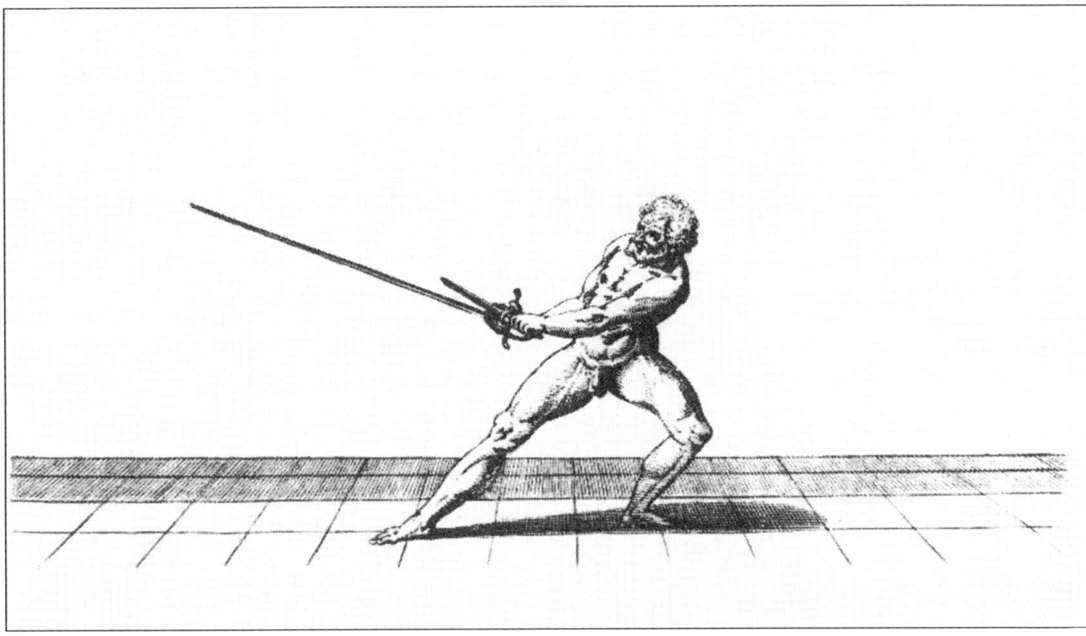

30 – *Guard with invitation to the left side of the body*

There are as many possible guards as there are positions of the sword, as we have said elsewhere; and each of them has a value to the man who understands tempo and measure.

He who forms his guards with artfulness even in the heat of battle will always deceive the opponent.

A Deceitful Guard that Leaves the Left Side of the Body Open

Deceitful guards are practically countless, although in my first book I will show only three; this will be enough to guide proficient fencers along the path to create as many as they want.

The correct (and first) way to form a deceitful guard is to leave one part of the body open, while keeping all the others well defended. This way, the opponent can attack you only in that one opening. In this example, you leave your left shoulder uncovered so that the opponent may attack you there. As he does so, he will be in danger: as soon as he launches his thrust or cut, you can parry and strike him in a single tempo, stepping forward with the foot that accompanies the sword while you parry.

These deceitful guards should be only employed by knowledgeable men—men who understand tempo and measure and who have a good degree of experience. There are many things that can be done from these guards, especially this first one. You can advance on the opponent and, as you arrive in measure (while the opponent is still waiting) you can strike him in whatever opening he has. And if the opponent strikes, you can do several things, such as parrying and striking in a single tempo, parrying and executing a feint, a pass—or anything you can do from another guard with which you have experience.

If the opponent, as you stand in guard, launches a two-tempi[28] attack on you, you can either parry and strike in one tempo or also in two—then immediately recover out of measure.

This guard is quite effective against both the proficient and the non-proficient. Your opening will be attacked, and you can easily and confidently parry and strike as described in the lessons of sword and dagger.

28 *Sconcertato,* literally "not in unison."

31 – Guard with invitation to the right side of the body

A Deceitful Guard that Leaves the Right Side of the Body Open

This is another deceitful guard, which as you see leaves the right side of the body open, while all other parts of your body remain covered. This way, the opponent can only attack your right shoulder, which you can parry with your sword or dagger, as you wish, while striking him by extending the right foot or with a pass.

This guard, too, gives you the opportunity to perform many feints. This type of guard is optimal against opponents who are eager to attack and don't have the patience to wait to strike in the correct tempo and measure. These opponents will gleefully attack whatever opening they see without considering what you could do to them—which is why they often end up in danger.

These guards are also good against the knowledgeable fencer, since you'll find it easier to see what to do. For instance, if the opponent performs a feint, you can more easily parry it than if you stood in a more covered guard. Full-intent thrusts can be easily parried by pulling the body back or, while parrying, turning the body—depending on how quick and long the opponent's thrusts will be.

32 – *Guard with invitation to the chest (between the weapons)*

A Deceitful Guard that Leaves the Chest Open

This guard leaves your chest open so that the opponent can neither attack you on the side of the sword nor on the side of the dagger—but can only attempt to strike you in the one opening, the chest. While he attacks, you can parry and strike him in a single tempo either in the right shoulder or in the face, since these are the closest openings. From this guard, you can also perform feints, pass, and do all the other things you have learned from the other guards.

This guard is also good against those who strike with full intent without feints. However, you should not use it against opponents who have an understanding of tempo and measure and who are equally skilled in the full-intent thrust and the feint. Instead, against this type of opponent you should stay covered behind your weapons, gain the opponent's sword with yours from out of measure, so you can parry and strike safely depending on the occasion.

33 – *Feint under the dagger, strike above the dagger*

The Feint of Sword and Dagger, to Strike above the Dagger

Knowledge of tempo and measure is the foundation of fencing; the cavazione and the feint are its ornament. The cavazione is performed wholly from the hand. Feinting is acting as if you are doing something and then not doing it; this action cannot take place without a cavazione. The cavazione is executed over or under the opponent's sword-hilt or dagger-point—both to the inside and to the outside. The feint cannot be addressed without also speaking of the cavazione.

The feint is a lethal deception. If you are gallant and proficient, you will find it almost impossible to defend against it; if you are not, get rid of the "almost." Here is how you can perform a feint to strike the opponent with a thrust to the chest or face.

Advance on the opponent with your sword under his dagger, while guarding his sword with your dagger. As you are in measure, deliver a full-intent thrust and recover. If you hit him, you don't need to do anything else. If he parries, advance on him once again, and when you are in measure, deliver a thrust without extending your front foot, and keeping your body steady and well-covered by the dagger. While the opponent attempts the parry, as he lowers the dagger, lift your sword by turning your hand—and at that point extend your step and your body and hit him in the chest or face, which he won't surely be able to defend against. This leads you to the position in the illustration. To make this succeed, perform the action with great speed, so that the opponent won't know if your movements are feints. Also, bear in mind that while you move your sword-point above his dagger, your sword moves forward with the cavazione; this way, the cavazione and the strike happen in one single tempo.

34 – Feint above the dagger, strike under the dagger

Feint of Sword and Dagger, to Strike in the Chest

This action follows the same rules as the previous one. The only difference is that this one ends with a strike under (not over) the opponent's dagger.

Start with your sword high and once you have advanced on the opponent, deliver a thrust above his dagger, lifting your sword-arm even more. This strike is called "*scannatura*[29] of the dagger." If he does not parry, you do not need to do anything else.

If he parries, the next time simply present your point to him in the same manner but without moving your feet, and while he attempts the parry, go with your sword-point under his dagger by turning your hand and hit him in the chest with an extension of your front foot. He will not be able to defend. Then, recover out of measure in the manner often described.

29 Scannatura literally means "throat-slitting." Used figuratively, like here and elsewhere in Italian swordsmanship, it often means a thrusting attack with the blade running closely parallel to a part of the opponent's body (such as the right arm) or one of his weapons (as in the example here).

35 – *Feint outside the sword, cavazione over the dagger-point*

Feint of Sword and Dagger, to Strike to the Face with a Cavazione over the Dagger-point

To easily strike the opponent in the face, you need to perform this feint, which is the most difficult but also the most beautiful. Advance on the opponent on the side of the sword, keeping your sword-point directed at his face on the right side; wait to see if he wants to attack or if he is just waiting to parry your attack.

If he is just waiting in guard, feint a thrust to his face. As he goes to the obedience with the dagger, perform the cavazione over his dagger-point (using only a turn of the hand) and strike him, since he will have opened himself up completely. After the strike, recover as often described.

36 – Sword-parry to the inside, with body-void

How to Use the Sword to Parry a Lunging Thrust while Bringing Your Body Back

Being good at parrying is one of the most useful and important things in our discipline. Let me show you three ways to parry a lunging thrust.

Stand in guard as described. Keep your sword and the body forward, presenting somewhat of an opening in the chest. This can be done either in measure or out of measure, but never inside the measure. If you are in measure and the opponent delivers a lunging thrust, bring your body back and parry with the sword as illustrated. In that tempo, you will be safe because you pull your body back and are far enough from the opponent's point that it won't reach you; but, having lowered his body, he will have disordered himself and will now be vulnerable—so you can strike him with an extension of your front foot, and recover as described.

Be advised that when you parry and when you get back, you stand steady on your feet.

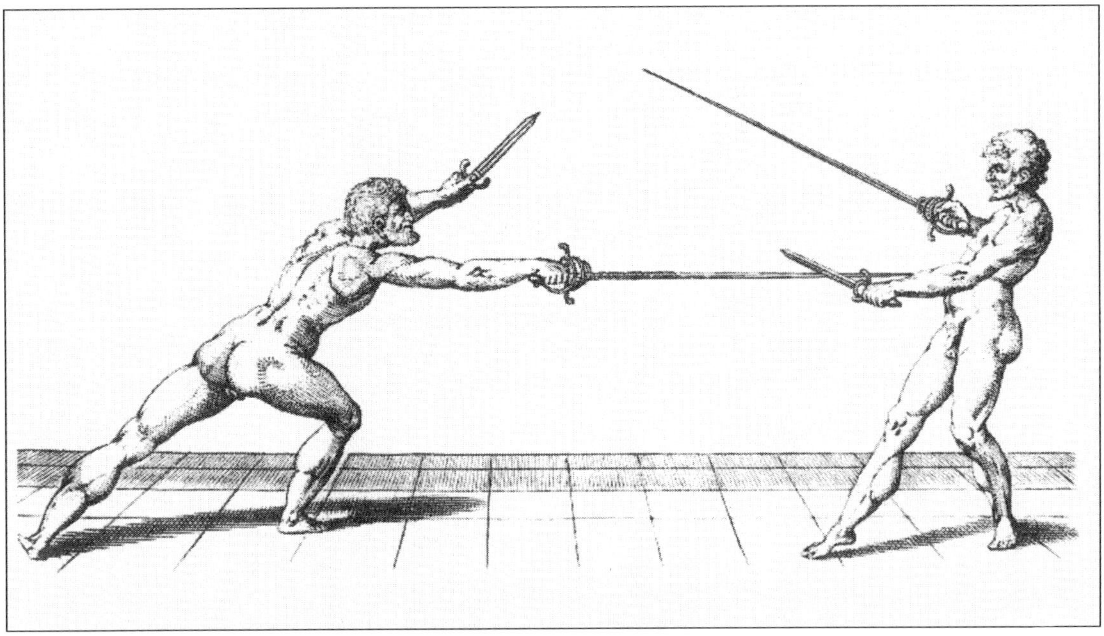

37 – Dagger-parry with body-void, for a two-tempi parry-riposte

How to Parry with the Dagger with Your Body Back

Stand in the guard often described, with your body deceitfully forward and the dagger guarding the opponent's sword. As you get in measure and the opponent delivers the thrust, use that tempo to parry with the dagger while bringing your body back and withdrawing your front foot and your sword, keeping the latter ready to strike (as pictured).

By keeping your feet steady and your sword free, you can do many things before he recovers in guard; he will give you the tempo to do so by virtue of his having lunged and lowered his body.

38 – *Dagger-parry, body-void and counterthrust to the chest*

Dagger-parry with the Body Back, with Simultaneous Sword-strike

In the last two illustrations, I had you parry with the dagger[30] and your body back, and then strike—i.e., employing two tempi, that is, one to parry, the other to strike. This time, I will show you how to parry and strike in one tempo. The reason for you to keep your body back is that you disorder the opponent and have a better chance to assess the situation.

Stand in the same sword-and-dagger guard I have described elsewhere, with the body bent forward. Once you are in measure, let the opponent attack; as he does so, you need to do three things in the same tempo. These are: parrying with the dagger, bringing your body back by pulling your front foot next to your rear foot (keeping your body bent); and extending your arm so as to deliver a thrust to his chest.

This manner of parrying and striking is so deceitful that he won't be able to defend.

Afterwards, recover safely out of measure as described elsewhere.

30 Actually, the sword had been used in the first of the two, the dagger in the second.

39 – Sword-parry and counterthrust

Sword-parry and Strike to the Face

This illustration shows a firm-footed thrust that is quite useful and stunning, as long as you practice it and you can perform it. Here is how it unfolds.

If the opponent delivers an imbroccata to your face or a *punta dritta,*[31] parry with the sword and, in the same tempo, direct your point to his face. He will be unable to parry with the dagger in the tempo while he attacks. This is because if he tries, his dagger would clash with his own sword, which won't prevent your point from hitting him in the face.

This lesson teaches exclusively a thrust to the face, because if you used it to attack his chest, he could parry your thrust with his dagger.

There is also an artful way to use this action to deceive good fencers; uncover the left side of your body, with your dagger low to invite an attack either to your face or above your dagger. The opponent will believe you will parry with your dagger, but you will instead do so with your sword, extending in the same tempo your right foot and straightening your point towards his face. Again, if he tries to parry with the dagger, he will only hit his own sword—this is why he will not be able to strike you or defend, as you see in the illustration. Once finished, recover out of measure as often described.

31 A high thrust with the hand in seconda.

40 – Sword-parry, dagger-thrust with a pass

The Pass in Sword and Dagger, to Grapple the Opponent and Strike Him in the Face with the Dagger

Grappling the opponent and striking him with the dagger can be done in different ways, depending on the situation. Many have no choice but to come to grapples, since the opponent is impulsive in his passing. Others pass out of sheer fury, lacking the patience to play at the point of the sword. Others yet use the pass as a deliberate technique that will enable them to strike the opponent with the dagger. Here is how this last type of passing attack is performed.

Set yourself in guard so as to leave the right side of your body wholly open, giving the opponent the opportunity to attack you with a full-intent thrust or cut. You will then parry his attack with the sword, pass forward and keep pressing on the opponent's sword so that your blade will end against his dagger-arm—as depicted. And since the opponent won't be able to move either of his weapons, you will be in the position to deliver as many dagger-strikes as you want.

Practice this action well, and it will be safe and dependable.

41 – Full-intent thrust to the right shoulder, outside the opponent's sword

The Thrust to the Right Shoulder in Sword and Dagger

A valiant fencer will never simply set himself in guard. Rather, he will stand out of measure and evaluate the opponent's own guard, then proceed slowly against him where he is most open; once in measure, he will strike the opponent as illustrated here, where the opening was the right shoulder.

In this case, advance on the opponent on the side of his sword; after seeing that your opponent is merely waiting, deliver a strong thrust as shown, turning your hand with the knuckles facing the opponent's sword (as pictured) and recovering out of measure as described.

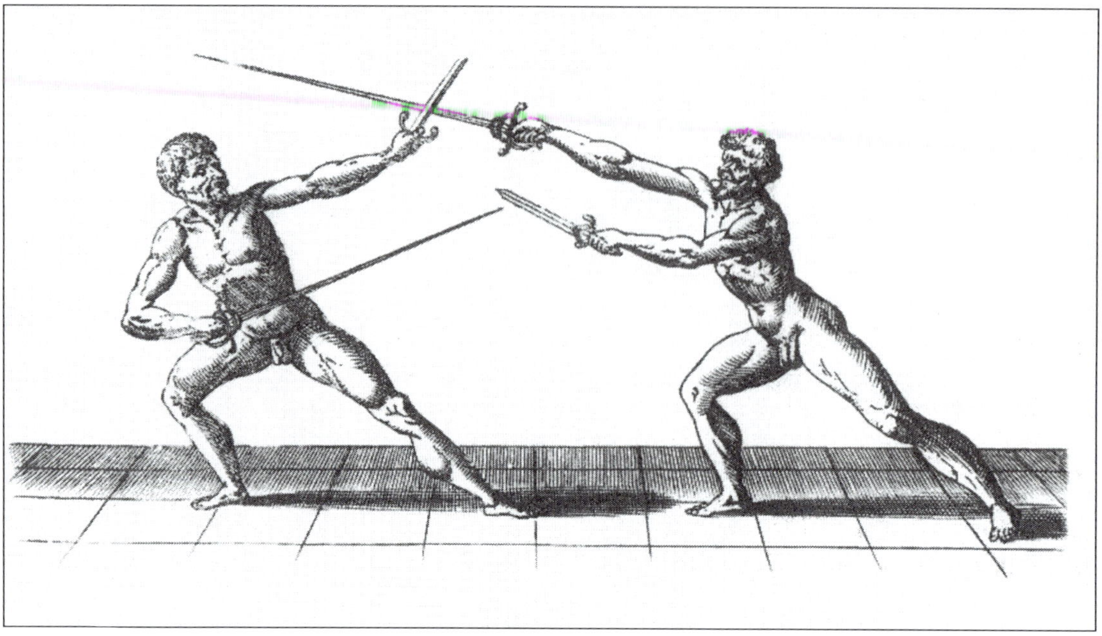

42 – Left-foot pass with cavazione to free his sword from the opponent's dagger (fencer on the left)

The Pass in Sword and Dagger

I am including this illustration only as an example in this first book of mine—God willing, I will write others in the future and deal with passing with sword and dagger. In this one, I have limited myself to the firm-footed attack in sword and dagger, also because if you know how to take the tempo, everything you can do firm-footed you will be able to do with a pass. After the pass, however, you need to know how to free your sword, as you see in this illustration, where the fencer on the left has passed and has freed his sword: now, he is safely able to deliver as many thrusts as he wants, since he is holding the opponent's sword with his dagger.

But if the opponent performs a cavazione, you need to follow his blade with your dagger while striking him with the sword with as many thrusts as you want—then recover out of measure.

Bear in mind that taking the tempo correctly and passing is all insufficient unless you are good at freeing your sword. After you pass, you are in danger even after striking the opponent, since he will also want to strike. There are fearless fencers who, after being hit, want to exact revenge and start throwing blows out of rage—blows that can leave you wounded or even dead. Similarly, if you pass and he parries your thrust, you will be in great danger if you cannot free your sword with a cavazione or if you cannot fight at the half-sword (as you see in the illustration) and then recover safely, as I will, God willing, speak of in other books.

THE END

Glossary

Advance – Moving both feet forward to get closer to the opponent.

Advantage of the sword – The situation you enjoy after having gained the opponent's sword.

Arms of the hilt – Two semicircular elements typically originating near the quillon-block of the hilt, and proceeding towards the sword-point on the same plane as the blade. Forward arm: the arm on the same side as the true edge, whose main function is to protect the index finger.

Beat – An action on the opponent's blade performed by delivering a cut to his debole with (typically) your mid-blade. It is designed to remove the opponent's point from your presence in preparation for a feint or a full-intent attack. A beat may be defeated with a cavazione.

Cavazione – A thrusting attack preceded by or incorporating a line-change, e.g., from the inside to the outside or vice-versa.

Contracavazione – 1. A thrusting attack that nullifies the opponent's cavazione by means of a cavazione of your own. Example: starting with you gaining the opponent's sword to the inside, he performs a cavazione to the outside and, in the same tempo, you perform one of your own, ending your action to the inside. 2. In Giganti's nomenclature, also the second cavazione in an action of feint by cavazione (not quite orthodox in Italian fencing terminology).

Counterattack – (Also, counter.) An attack performed in the tempo of the opponent's attack. It must incorporate a parry, a void or both.

Counter-guard, counter-posture – In Giganti, the position of your body and weapon(s) after you gain the opponent's sword.

Cut – An attack that uses the shearing power of the sword's edge to inflict a wound.

Debole – The half of the blade closer to the point, whose function is primarily offensive.

Double hit – A faulty action resulting in both fencers hitting one-another simultaneously or almost simultaneously.

Feint – 1. A simulated attack designed to provoke a parry, so you can defeat the parry with a cavazione and hit the opponent in the opening he creates. 2. Any simulated action—including a retreat, a parry, etc.—design to provoke a specific reaction from the opponent.

Firm-footed attack – 1. An attack accompanied by lunging footwork. 2. An attack that does not incorporate the motion of either foot. It stands in contrast to a passing attack.

Full-intent attack – An attack not intended as the first motion of a feint, but as a fully-committed attack.

Forte – The half of the blade closer to the swordsman's hand, whose function is primarily defensive.

Gaining the sword – Situating your blade so that it crosses over the opponent's, your forte on his debole, and prevents him from attacking without a cavazione. In Giganti, this action is always performed with the true edge.

Glide – A thrusting attack with opposition in which your forte glides along the opponent's debole. It is typically a true-edge action.

Handle – The part of the sword-hilt consisting of a flattened cylinder generally made of wood wrapped in wire. It is the element around which the middle, ring and little fingers are wrapped while gripping the sword.

Imbroccata – A thrust with the hand in prima, typically a descending thrust.

Incascio – The part of the hilt between the arms of the hilt and the ricasso.

Inquartata – 1. A thrusting attack or counterattack with the hand in quarta, and the left foot circling behind the right, thereby removing the body from the line of the opponent's attack. 2. A thrusting attack with a marked opposition to the inside.

Invitation – A deliberate opening offered to the opponent to induce him to attack.

Lunging thrust - A thrusting attack that incorporates an extension of the right foot, while the left remains anchored. It is classified as a firm-footed attack.

Mandritto – A cutting attack delivered right to left.

Measure – The distance between two opposing fencers. In the 17th century, it was classified in slightly different ways. The following is what Giganti uses. In measure: a distance from the opponent from which you can strike him with a single motion (typically, with a lunging attack). Out of measure: a distance from the opponent from which you need at least one advancing step before being able to strike him. Inside the measure, or within measure: being closer to the opponent than when you are in measure.

Obedience – An opponent goes to the obedience when he responds to your action with the action (typically a parry) that you intended to provoke. In this sense, he is obeying you.

Opposition – An obtuse angle formed between the sword-arm and the sword in the course of an attack or counterattack, designed to exclude the opponent's weapon from your presence. Note: as a term, it did not become the norm until the 18th century, although the concept existed and was emphasized long before, by authors such as Giganti. Example in layman's terms: to form opposition to the outside in the course of a thrusting attack, extend your arm forward and slightly to your right, forming an obtuse angle with your blade as your point is directed towards the opponent. This will ensure that your hilt and the forte of your blade keep the opponent's point safely away from you.

Parity of swords – A situation in the course of an action when the opposing swords end up with neither enjoying a mechanical advantage. Example: you launch a strong thrust, the opponent foils it with a strong parry.

Parry – A defensive action in which the sword, a companion weapon or the left hand is used to deflect or stop the opponent's incoming blade.

Pass – 1. An attack in which the rear foot ends up as the forward foot. 2. A form of footwork in which each foot is placed forward ahead of the other (advancing pass) or backward behind the other (retreating pass).

Possession of the sword – See advantage of the sword.

Presenting the point – Straightening your arm at full extension, point in line, to threaten the opponent or to induce him to gain your sword.

Punta dritta – A thrust with the hand in seconda, typically to the outside.

Quillons – The hilt's crossguard, i.e., two lengths of steel proceeding more or less at right angles with the edges of the blade. Forward quillon: the quillon on the side of the true edge. Quillon block: the V-shaped block between the quillons, whose apex points towards the sword's point.

Recovery – Getting back in guard after an attack. In Giganti, it typically incorporates a simultaneous retreat out of measure.

Retreat – Moving both feet backward to get farther from the opponent.

Ricasso – The thick part of the sword's blade going from the quillon block to a few inches past the hilt.

Riverso – A cutting attack delivered left to right.

Simple parry – A parry that does not incorporate a simultaneous counterattack.

Stance – The distance between your feet while in guard.

Stoccata – 1. A generic name for a thrust. 2. A thrust to the inside line, as opposed to a *punta dritta*.

Tempo – 1. A unit of fencing time. 2. A motion made by a fencer while in measure, that gives the opponent an opportunity to attack or gain an advantage. 3. An opportunity to strike the opponent.

Thrust – An attack that uses the penetrative power of the sword to inflict a wound.

Void – An evasive action, typically of the body, designed to avoid getting hit by the opponent's attack.

9780982591123